CRAVING COUNSELLING

FOR PATIENTS, RELATIVES AND HEALTHCARE PROVIDERS

CRAVING COUNSELLING

FOR PATIENTS, RELATIVES AND HEALTHCARE PROVIDERS

HEMANG C. PAJWANI

Worldwide Published by

Pendown Press

PENDOWN PRESS

An ISO 9001 & ISO 14001 Certified Co.,

Regd. Office: 2525/193, 1st Floor, Onkar Nagar-A,
Tri Nagar, Delhi-110035

Ph.: 09350849407, 09312235086

E-mail: info@pendownpress.com

Branch Office: 1A/2A, 20, Hari Sadan, Ansari Road,
Daryaganj, New Delhi-110002

Ph.: 011-45794768

Website: PendownPress.com

First Edition: 2021

ISBN: 978-93-90828-81-4

Layout and Cover Designed by Pendown Graphics Team

Printed and Bound in India by Thomson Press India Ltd.

DEDICATION

I dedicate this book to all those patients, their family members and also the healthcare providers who refuse to accept depression.

CONTENTS

The Beginning i

Introduction: How can you be a real life hero? iv

Acknowledgement vii

KNOWLEDGE BYTE –1

Palliative care Overview 1

KNOWLEDGE BYTE –2

Need of Counselling for Patients, Family Members and Healthcare Providers 8

KNOWLEDGE BYTE –3

Health Insurance overview 20

KNOWLEDGE BYTE –4

Rights and responsibilities of Patients 26

Conclusion 29

Annexure 30

Sources 33

THE BEGINNING

Hello My Name is Hemang Pajwani, an Instrumentation Engineer by education,. entrepreneur by Profession and by passion "A volunteer Platelet donor", a Motivational Speaker for "donating Blood and platelets."

In 1993, I completed my Graduation in Instrumentation Engineering and joined a job with a handsome salary. Suddenly, my father had a massive heart-attack in 1995, but by the grace of God he survived, but could not resume our family business of "Pharmaceutical Distribution in Mumbai" on a regular basis. Ultimately I left the job of my engineering field and joined shoulder to shoulder with my elder brother for Family business. And now I am a successful businessman in the Pharmaceutical Industry.

During Engineering, I studied in Hostel and one fine night, when I was sleeping in my room with my roommates, one unknown person knocked on our room's door and asked me to join him at the hospital. I was shocked and asked "Who are you? Why should I join you? " But, after watching my Hostel Dean with him I was relaxed. Later, he explained to me the complete scenario and I understood the value of Blood donation for the first time ever in my life. One 7 years' old baby girl was suffering with Thalassemia and she was in urgent need of blood from an "O negative blood group donor."I remembered that at the time of college admission I had mentioned my blood group in the form. After donating Blood I was feeling proud of myself for helping someone, whom I was not knowing and might never meet ever. At that time I came to know one of the secrets of becoming "A real-life hero."

And from that day, my journey as a Volunteer Blood Donor, started and I committed myself to give blood donations regularly. But due to the "O negative Blood group" I can not donate without an emergency. Up to April 2013 I have donated blood maximum 5 times only.

In April 2013 I met Mr. Mehul Doshi through our common friend Mr. Bakulesh Thakkar. He guided me and suggested that I should start a Platelet Donation in Tata Memorial Hospital, Mumbai, the most leading and reputed hospital for Cancer treatment In India. It was the first time I came to know about the platelet donation and my journey of Platelet Donation started since 15/04/2013. Till the date of the publication of this book (31/01/2021) I have donated Platelets 168 times and the journey will continue till I can able to maintain good health (does not get diagnosed as diabetic, or some other diseases that make me unfit to donate blood) or law of India permits.

Blood is needed to treat the accident victims, cancer patients, trauma induced surgeries, orthopedic/cardiovascular surgeries, pregnancy complications and in many more medical emergencies also. Platelets are used for cancer, trauma, burn and surgery patients to assist with blood clotting and stop internal and external bleeding. It is useful in treating Dengue patients also. Even in some incidences operations/surgeries get delayed due to non-availability of Blood/platelets.

In the current scenario awareness of Blood/Platelets donation and its need are not much explored. Ultimately it's always a shortage of Blood/Platelets to treat patients. One of the biggest challenges is the shelf-life of blood and Platelets are 42 days and 5 days respectively. Means, once Blood/Platelets get donated it should be consumed before it gets expired.

Its simple solution is to spread awareness of platelet donation and youngsters should come forward to donate as and when required. As of now we have almost 700 volunteer donors in Tata Memorial Hospital who regularly donate platelets and as of now 85% of the total need of Tata Hospital is fulfilled by volunteer donors only. (as per July 2020 Records)

I am giving you Bold promise that "if all the healthy citizens of India come forward to donate blood/platelets there will be zero death, no delay in operations due to lack of blood/platelets.

We can be the First country in the world who might be able to fulfill complete blood/platelets needs of the country. In the whole world India can be known/recognized as "Country of the Millions of real-life heroes."

And now I am on a mission to make India "the country of the Millions of Real-life heroes" by 2025 where there will be zero incident when any operations/surgeries will be delayed due to unawareness of Healthcare Education and non-availability of Blood/platelets.

INTRODUCTION

How can you be a real life hero?

Contrary to the popular belief, you need not be a spiderman or shaktiman, nor you need to wear a cap, or even be a politician. Simply put, if your acts are heroic, you will emerge as a hero for sure.

1. **Let go of the ego of yours:** The first and foremost thing that you should do is to let off your ego. You should not attach a certain price with yourself. Make yourself available for the right cause and right people, without attaching a Self Tag.
2. **Initiate the particular shift you wish to determine:** Thought without action is like abortion. If you are determined for something, say plantation drive in your area, some economic activities that will provide mass employment, some move for the environment, etc., do not move about the right moment or something called "favourable condition."

3. **Take responsibility for your failure and give credit to someone else for the success:** Initiate something big that will create a big impact on the people around you. Pursue your plan consistently, learn how to take optimum use of the people around you, try to achieve the desired outcome in a specified amount of time. If the plan turns out to be a fiasco, come forward, take the responsibility (of your failure). But, when your plan becomes successful, take credit to someone else in your group.
4. **Be prepared to act when others are actually passive:** Do not act like average. Be the front runner. When you believe in something, stick to it. Do not let your determination die down, simply because most of the people are opposing it. If you can clearly see you goal, rest assured, you will achieve it. Mind, at the initial phases, you will find most of the people talking exactly the opposite. But, as you refuse to budge, and keep on doing the things, uninterruptedly, you will achieve both—the target as well as the confidence of the people.
5. **Perform arbitrary actions associated with kindness:** The act of kindness is independent of an auspicious moment. If you see politicians' kindness related actions at the time of election, or a famous person in your area distributing clothes on his or her birthday, do not get the impression (wrong) that kindness' actions are occasion-bound. Just start doing acts of kindness. Arrange tuition fees for a poor student, buy a noon-time meal for your needy rather than offering income, take an aged neighbor to a healthcare appointment, donate blood/platelets.

6. **Do not Advertise your Accomplishments:** You may find it paradoxical, but it is irrefutably true. You need not do anything for your society with a motive. You should not think like "As I want to be a hero, I must give charity, actions related to kindness and advertise every feet of accomplishment." Instead, think like "I am committed to the welfare of my people. I will keep on doing good things, irrespective of what people think about me. For me, kindness is not an investment. It is true." If you evolve your mind and become altruist by nature, rest assure, you will emerge as a hero.

   Donate Blood/Platelets: Educate people about how their blood/platelets can help save lives. Set an example of your own. Donate blood. Educate near and dear one about the fundamentals of healthcare and stand beside them whenever they are in need.

ACKNOWLEDGEMENT

I am grateful to Mr. Ajay Pathak, who is a "Cancer Survival" and showed the importance of Counselling for simple teachings and insights into how to live more and more happy, meaningful and fulfilling life. It has been his guidance which has served as the main source of inspiration for the creation and development of this book.

This book will prepare you for success, suggest the various ways to recover from setbacks and achieve balance, success and helps register growth towards personal excellence.

(Nothing depends on LUCK. Everything depends on WORK because even LUCK has to WORK)

KNOWLEDGE BYTE-1

PALLIATIVE CARE OVERVIEW

What is Palliative Care?

Palliative care is specialized medical care that focuses on providing patients relief from pain and other symptoms of a serious illness, no matter the diagnosis or stage of disease. Palliative care teams aim to improve the quality of life for both patients and their families. This form of care is offered alongside curative or other treatments you may be receiving.'

Palliative care is provided by a team of doctors, nurses and other specially trained people. They work with you, your family and your other doctors to provide an extra layer of support that complements your ongoing care.

Palliative care is actually a new medical specialty that has recently emerged – and no, it's not the same as hospice. It doesn't serve only the dying. Instead, it focuses more broadly on improving life and providing comfort to people of all ages with serious, chronic, and life-threatening illnesses.

Why is it done?

Palliative care may be offered to people of any age who have a serious or life-threatening illness. It can help adults and children living with illnesses such as:

- Cancer
- Blood and bone marrow disorders requiring stem cell transplant
- Heart disease
- Cystic fibrosis
- Dementia
- End-stage liver disease
- Kidney failure
- Lung disease
- Parkinson's disease
- Stroke

Symptoms that may be improved by palliative care include:

- Pain
- Nausea or vomiting
- Anxiety or nervousness
- Depression or sadness
- Constipation
- Difficulty breathing
- Anorexia
- Fatigue
- Trouble sleeping

When Is Palliative Care Appropriate?

If you've been diagnosed with a serious, long-lasting disease or with a life-threatening illness, palliative care can make your life – and the lives of those who care for you – much easier.

Palliative care can be performed along with the care you receive from your primary doctors.

With palliative care, there is a focus on relieving pain and other troubling symptoms and meeting your emotional, spiritual, and practical needs. In short, this new medical specialty aims to improve your quality of life – however you define that for yourself.

Your palliative care providers will work with you to identify and carry out your goals: symptom relief, counseling, spiritual comfort, or whatever enhances your quality of life. Palliative care can also help you to understand all of your treatment options.

One of the strengths of palliative care is recognition of the human side of illness. In a 2011 survey of palliative care patients, they mentioned these particular needs: "being recognized as a person," "having a choice and being in control," "being connected to family and the world outside," "being spiritually connected," and "physical comfort."

Be assured that you may receive palliative care at the same time that you pursue a cure for your illness. You won't be required to give up your regular doctors or treatments or hope for a cure.

When can I start palliative care?

You may start palliative care at any stage of your illness, even as soon as you receive a diagnosis and begin treatment. You don't have to wait until your disease has reached an advanced stage or when you're in the final months of life. In fact, the earlier you start palliative care, the better.

How do you prepare?

Here's some information to help you get ready for your first consultation appointment.

- Bring a list of symptoms you're experiencing. Note specifically what makes the symptoms better or worse and whether they affect your ability to go about your daily activities.
- Bring a list of medications and supplements you use.
- Consider bringing a family member or friend with you to the appointment.
- Bring any advance directives and living wills you've completed.

What you can expect?

Palliative care is an approach to care that you may want to access at any stage of a serious illness. It helps you manage symptoms and address concerns that matter most to you. You may consider palliative care when you have questions about:

- What to expect with your care plan and how to tailor it to what matters most to you
- What programs and resources are available to support you throughout your illness
- Your treatment options and their pros and cons
- Making decisions in line with your personal values and goals

Your first meeting may take place while you're in the hospital or in an outpatient clinic. Research indicates that early use of palliative care services can improve the quality of life for patients with serious illness, decrease depression and anxiety, increase patient and family satisfaction with care, and, in some cases, even extend survival.

Questions to Ask Your Palliative Care Team

Here are questions to ask your palliative care team, according to the Center to Advance Palliative Care:

- What can I expect from palliative care?
- Where will I receive my care (for example, in the hospital, home, nursing home, or hospice?)
- Who will be part of my palliative care team?
- What are your recommendations for my care?
- What will you do if I experience severe pain or uncomfortable symptoms?
- How will you communicate with my other doctors?
- What decisions will my family or I need to make?
- Will you be able to help explain the issues involved in making these decisions?
- Will you communicate candidly about my illness with me and my family?
- What support will you provide to my family or caregivers?
- Will you still be involved in my care when I'm discharged from the hospital?
- Can you explain the difference between hospice and palliative care?

- Will you still be available to me throughout my care, including hospice, if needed?
- What resources do you recommend for me to learn more about palliative care?

What happens during the consultation?

Your palliative care team will talk with you about your symptoms, current treatments, and how this illness is affecting you and your family. You and your palliative care team make a plan to prevent and ease suffering and improve your daily life. This plan will be carried out in coordination with your primary care team in a way that works well with any other treatment you're receiving.

What happens after the consultation?

Your palliative care plan is designed to fit your life and needs. It may include elements such as:

Symptom management. Your palliative care plan will include steps to address your symptoms and improve your comfort and well-being. The care team will answer questions you may have, such as whether your pain medicines will affect treatments you're receiving from your primary care doctor.

Support and advice. Palliative care services include support for the many difficult situations and decisions you and your family make when you're facing a serious illness or approaching the end of life.

You and your family may talk with a palliative care social worker, chaplain or other team member about stress, spiritual questions, financial concerns or how your family will cope if a loved one dies. The palliative care specialists may offer guidance or connect you with community resources.

Care techniques that improve your comfort and sense of well-being. These may include breathing techniques, healing touch, visualization or simply listening to music with headphones.

Referrals. Your palliative care clinician may refer you to other doctors: for example, specialists in psychiatry, pain medicine or integrative medicine.

Advance care planning. A palliative care team member can talk with you about goals and wishes for your care. This information could then be used to help you develop a living will, advance directive and a health care power of attorney.

Your palliative care team collaborates with your regular doctors to ensure your care is well-coordinated.

Conclusion

Many people associate palliative care with end-of-life care. Although all end-of-life care includes palliative care, not all palliative care is end-of-life care.

The palliative care team works alongside the doctors working to extend your life and, if possible, to cure your illness. By relieving your symptoms, the palliative care team may actually help you improve.

This approach to care is for anyone with a serious, life-threatening illness, whether they're expected to live for years or for months or for just days.

KNOWLEDGE BYTE–2

NEED OF COUNSELLING FOR PATIENTS, FAMILY MEMBERS AND HEALTHCARE PROVIDERS

The purpose of this knowledge byte is to help you understand how professional counselling and support can help you cope with cancer. Very often, we are not aware of how deeply a disease affects the human spirit and emotional health. The information contained here is intended to lighten the burden of people who are living with cancer, and their families, by describing what psychosocial support can offer. In this way, we hope to give realistic and useful information about getting help with the emotional distress that is a normal part of the experience of having cancer.

The difficult reality is that a cancer diagnosis can be as devastating emotionally as it is physically. It is my hope that this knowledge byte will give all cancer patients and families the know-how to reach out for support when it's needed.

Types of Counselling

Counselling is part of an integrated team approach to treating patient needs in a holistic way. Different individuals may be available for counselling depending on the services in the community and your level of need. Most cancer centres offer individual counselling by psychologists, psychiatrists, social workers and chaplains, as well as pain and symptom management nurse and physician specialists. Counsellors do much of their work one-on-one with patients, but they also work with families. Some departments offer group counselling, or peer support groups led by a trained professional. Dieticians who will customize a nutrition plan to your individual needs may also work as part of the counselling team. Advanced practice nurses with specialized knowledge and skill related to cancer also provide counselling.

The counsellors in settings where cancer treatments are given are required to have specific psychosocial oncology training. Counsellors understand the physical and biological aspects of cancer treatment, and their specific impact on your overall well-being.

The Counselling Process

If you've never had an experience with professional counselling, you may wonder how it works. Most counsellors use a fairly well defined three-stage process. The first stage involves exploring and identifying concerns. The next stage is about understanding how these concerns relate to your life, how you think, and your life history. The third stage focuses on taking action about your concerns, or learning to live with them in a different way. Here's a little more detail on what happens at each stage.

Exploration

You begin counselling by telling your story. Cancer may be changing many things in your life. You may be able to cope with some of them; others may be beyond your coping ability. The stress of cancer may affect your personal relationships, your sense of self. You may have other worries, and as you struggle to deal with these changes, intense emotions may surface. The exploration process helps you become aware of all the issues you are dealing with and their place and importance in your life.

Understanding

The next stage of counselling is to understand how you feel, think, react and behave in relation to your concerns. Getting a sense of both what is working and what is not can help you to regain a sense of control. Practical issues are often easier to understand and resolve than deeply felt internal ones. However, examining and working through your feelings and behaviours promotes a clearer understanding of what is positive and health promoting for you, and what is not.

Action

After issues become clearer, you may decide if, when and where to take action to reduce difficulties or regain control in a situation that may seem overwhelming. Action can take many forms. Here are a few examples:

- Making a list of questions to ask your doctor
- Taking an active part in treatment decisions

- Accepting help and asking for support from family and friends
- Setting achievable goals and planning how to reach them
- Re-establishing a sense of meaning and purposefulness in life
- Learning new skills to cope with your fears and stresses
- Changing patterns of living or relationships that are unsatisfying

Counselling and Confidentiality

All health professionals in India are bound by a code of ethics and legislation that guarantees confidentiality. Confidentiality means that your discussions with a counsellor will not be shared with others. The exceptions occur when patients threaten to harm themselves or others, or when incidents of child abuse are disclosed. In these cases health professionals are legally bound to ensure that people are protected. This may require informing authorities.

Do patient Need Professional Support?

Self-Assessment Questionnaire For Patients

The following questionnaire may help you determine whether you might benefit from professional counselling. Every patient experiences some of these symptoms; there are no right or wrong answers.

During the past two weeks:

1. I have felt anxious or worried about cancer and the treatment I am receiving.

Not at all	1	2	3	4	5	All the time

2. I have felt depressed or discouraged.

Not at all	1	2	3	4	5	All the time

3. I have been irritable or unusually angry and I have not controlled it well.

Not at all	1	2	3	4	5	All the time

4. My sleeping habits have changed.

Not at all	1	2	3	4	5	All the time

5. I have experienced a change in my appetite.

Not at all	1	2	3	4	5	Very Much

6. I have had difficulty concentrating at work or at home, or on routine things such as reading the newspaper or watching television.

Not at all	1	2	3	4	5	Very Much

7. Cancer and its treatment have interfered with my daily activities.

Not at all	1	2	3	4	5	Very Much

8. Cancer and its treatment have interfered with my family or social life.

Not at all	1	2	3	4	5	Very Much

9. Cancer and its treatment have interfered with my sexual life.

Not at all	1	2	3	4	5	Very Much

10. Pain and discomfort have caused me to limit my activities.

Not at all	1	2	3	4	5	Very Much

11. Cancer has caused physical, emotional or financial hardship for me.

Not at all	1	2	3	4	5	Very Much

12. Cancer and its treatment have caused changes in my physical appearance and this concerns me.

Not at all	1	2	3	4	5	Very Much

13. I have had difficulty coping with the stress I have experienced.

Not at all	1	2	3	4	5	Very Much

14. My quality of life during the past two weeks has been:

Not at all	1	2	3	4	5	Very Poor

If you find that many of your answers are in columns four or five, you may be experiencing significant distress and should consider discussing your feelings with a counsellor.

Self-Assessment Questionnaire for Family and Caregivers

The following questionnaire may help you as a family member or caregiver to determine whether you might benefit from professional counselling.

1. I feel anxious or worried about my loved one's cancer diagnosis/treatment.

Not at all	1	2	3	4	5	Very Much

2. I feel depressed or discouraged.

Not at all	1	2	3	4	5	Very Much

3. I have been irritable or unusually angry and I have not controlled it well.

Not at all	1	2	3	4	5	Very Much

4. My sleeping habits have changed.

Not at all	1	2	3	4	5	Very Much

5. I have experienced a change in my appetite.

Not at all	1	2	3	4	5	Very Much

6. I have had difficulty concentrating at work, home or school, or on routine things such as reading the newspaper or watching television.

Not at all	1	2	3	4	5	Very Much

7. My loved one's diagnosis/treatment interferes with my daily activities.

Not at all	1	2	3	4	5	Very Much

8. My loved one's diagnosis/treatment interferes with my family or social life.

Not at all	1	2	3	4	5	Very Much

9. My loved one's diagnosis/treatment interferes with sexual life.

Not at all	1	2	3	4	5	Very Much

10. My loved one's diagnosis has caused financial hardship to our family.

Not at all	1	2	3	4	5	Very Much

11. I have difficulty keeping up with my caregiving activities.

Not at all	1	2	3	4	5	Very Much

12. I have difficulty coping with the stress that the entire family is experiencing.

Not at all	1	2	3	4	5	Very Much

Everyone experiences some of these symptoms, to varying degrees, part of the time. If you find that many of your answers are in columns four or five, and you are having difficulty dealing with your situation on your own, you may be experiencing significant distress. Please do not hesitate to discuss your feelings with a psychosocial oncology counsellor.

How Counselling Helps Patients

The greatest benefit of psychosocial care is that patients and families may experience a significant improvement in quality of life. Without emotional support, people can struggle unguided with issues of their own mortality, with complex questions about quality and quantity of life, and with the burden of coping with treatments and suffering, both physical and emotional. Through counselling, you may be better equipped to enjoy a fulfilling and productive life.

The experience of cancer can have the effect of putting a magnifying glass over one's life: it tends to bring out the good, amplifying the strong supportive bonds with friends and family. However, the impact of the illness can also exaggerate the difficulties of everyday life, related, for instance, to marital problems or to family communications issues. These may add to the considerable anxiety of living with the cancer itself.

Patients who receive emotional support are better equipped to cope with the relationship problems and the fear, depression and anxiety that are a normal part of dealing with cancer. Counselling can help to ease tensions within the family, and help with the complicated task of getting financial aid, making it easier for the person to get on with the important job of coping with the disease and its treatment.

For many people, one of the greatest benefits of counselling is that it is an opportunity to have their problems given individual attention. Counsellors have a deep sensitivity to the fact that the life of every person with cancer is unique. Counselling work is about tailoring an individualized approach to each situation.

The Benefits of Counselling for Family and Caregivers

The emotional distress experienced by family and caregivers can be just as intense or even more intense than the patient's. Nearly half of all caregivers experience some form of depression, as well as physical and emotional exhaustion brought on by the intensity of providing care. Professional counselling can lessen this distress, from the early stages of diagnosis and treatment, right through grieving and bereavement in the case of loss of a loved one.

Many family members consider one of counselling's biggest advantages the fact that they can express pent-up feelings and emotions which are often tightly under control when they're with the patient or other family members. Often, families and caregivers feel helpless when faced with the serious illness of a loved one. They aren't sure what to do, what actions or words are appropriate. Professional support helps to overcome these feelings of helplessness, to give strategies to cope with feelings, and a realistic idea about what can and cannot be done in any given situation.

Often families and caregivers want to be very positive, caring and upbeat. This can place further strain on the family, as it allows no room for the sadness that is a very real part of everyone's experience of cancer. Family members and caregivers often react to their own distress by trying to be proactive; however, if their ideas don't mesh with wishes of the patient this can be a source of tension. The lack of meaningful communication can leave the patient feeling misunderstood and angry, and the family member feeling unappreciated and isolated. Counselling can be useful to work out some of these issues and ease family tensions, and play a very important role in aiding communication between patient, caregiver and family.

Concluding, counselling can help Family members and caregivers to manage their emotional distress, including:

1. Young children with a parent with cancer
2. Adult children with parents with cancer
3. Children with cancer

KNOWLEDGE BYTE-3

HEALTH INSURANCE OVERVIEW

9 Point Checklist That Helps To Buy Right Health Insurance

There are many health insurance options available with a wide range of benefits. You should focus on factors such as benefits and conditions that limit the benefits while choosing the plan that protects your finances in emergencies.

Choosing the right individual health plan from the plethora of health insurance options available today is sure not easy to find. Keeping in mind the strenuous lifestyle we lead and rising medical cost, health insurance is a crucial tool today. Therefore, ignoring the need for health insurance or just selecting any plan without an informed decision could lead your life to the breadline.

Today, with medical cost at an all-time high, emergencies like sickness, disease and accidents resulting in prolonged hospitalization, can leave you in severe financial crisis unless you have a comprehensive medical insurance policy which takes care of all your required expenses. So how do you choose a plan that's perfectly suitable for you and your family?

There are a lot of factors to consider when choosing an insurance plan, most importantly: what your health care needs are, and what you can afford to spend? Once you are aware of your financial strength, the next step is to identify the "ought-to-have" with anticipating certain medical needs. With the right insurance, you could save thousands, perhaps even tens of thousands, if you or a family member gets sick.

Here are some critical clauses that needs your attention to detail while buying a health insurance policy:

1. **Sum Insured Limits:** The main limit in health insurance is the sum insured. Any medical expenses incurred over and above the sum insured is not payable. It is advisable to take adequate cover from an early age, particularly because it may not be easy to increase the sum insured after a claim occurs or when the age increases.
2. **Individual/Floater Policies:** Most buyers often struggle to make a decision on whether to buy an "individual" policy for each family member or a "family floater policies". While an individual policy works best in all situations, it can be an expensive option. The family floater plan on the other hand offers flexibility in terms of utilizing the overall insurance coverage among the family as a group. While an individual opts for a family floater cover, the sum insured opted should be sufficiently high considering a situation where more than one person in a family needs hospitalisation in the same year.

3. **Extent of coverage:** When you are paying for a comprehensive cover, it is important to make sure that the risk covered is comprehensive as well. One should not buy a plan just because it's cheaper than the rest but should be measured in terms of premium versus benefit comparison. Benefits such as pre and post hospitalisation, Day care procedures, OPD cover, Maternity extensions or ambulance service, should be taken into consideration.

4. **Waiting period for pre-existing disease exclusions:** Many individuals have health related problems that exist before you apply for a health insurance policy or enroll in a new health plan. Pre-existing conditions impose a waiting period which is also called the cooling period. Therefore, apart from the insurance premium being charged by various insurers, you also need to compare the waiting periods stipulated in the policies for covering pre-existing ailments. Some policies specify a waiting period of two years, while in case of some, it could extend to four years. Similarly there are waiting periods for certain listed conditions like Hysterectomies, Cataract, Kidney Stones and Knee Replacement surgeries which may again vary from one year to four years and these also need to be compared. One should not be discouraged with this clause even if certain ailments are not covered.

5. **Any internal sub limits like room rent restrictions**, sub limits on specific procedures.

   In order to avoid inflated charges that hospitals levy on patients with an insurance cover, some policies have sub-limits on room rents or certain procedures and this becomes the most critical feature when evaluating a health insurance policy. Typically the insurer places two kinds of limits, on the hospital room rent and the liability for specific diseases.

Classically the room rent expenses are capped at 1% of the sum assured for a day, while ICU charges have a ceiling of 2% of the sum assured. Plans free of sub-limits are preferred as it prevents surprises at the time of claims. These sub-limits are generally seen in plans with lower overall sums insured.

6. **Deductibles/Copayments:** Sub-limits can also take the form of co-payments, where the insurer will be asked to pay a predetermined percentage of the claim amount or deductibles, where the insurer will have a cut-off cost which you will have to bear and the insurer will come into the picture only when the bill goes beyond this limit. It is advisable to go for plans that come devoid of restrictive options, such as co-payments, limits on room rents and treatment-specific limits. They may cost a little more but evade financial risk during emergencies.
7. **List of Exclusions:** While your health insurance policy can provide relief in times of emergencies, there may also be times of trouble, in case you are not aware about the ailments that are covered and those that aren't. It is important to know the list of exclusions in your health insurance policy, to avoid instances when you end up paying additionally for a service already covered in your policy or in the worst case scenario, post treatment you realise that your policy did not cover the treatment of that particular illness.

8. **In house claims servicing or use of TPA and service levels/market feedback:** It is important to know whether the insurance company has its own in-house servicing unit or uses a TPA for servicing the policies.

   Insurance companies having their in-house servicing units have a better turnaround time for claims servicing as well as cashless processing.

   A hospital or medical institution which has an agreement with the insurance company or TPA (Third Party Administrator) to provide cash less treatment, is a network hospital. While buying a health plan, make sure of the proximity of the network hospital from your place of residence or work. Opt for an insurer who has more network hospitals in geographical locations where you are likely to need medical care. Ensure that the facilities and repute of the hospitals in the network are worthy.

9. **Reputation of the company in the market and among providers.** Traditionally, we all are inclined to go for plans that our friends and family suggest as we trust their experience and judgment. But the market is flooded with products and marketing gimmicks to lure customers. While deciding on a health plan, it's important to conduct a due diligence on the insurance company – keeping track of how smooth their claim settlement is, how many claims have been settled, time – efficient, well networked.

   With splurging medical costs across the globe, a medical policy can help you stay more relaxed for finances during emergencies and also entitle you to impressive tax benefits. On the face of it, all policies may look identical and therefore reading the fine prints is vital.

How to claim for health insurance?

Formalities for a health insurance claim

You can make a claim under a Health insurance policy in two ways:

1. Cashless basis and
2. Reimbursement basis

On a Cashless basis

For a claim on a cashless basis, your treatment must be only at a network hospital of the Third Party Administrator (TPA) who is servicing your policy. You have to seek authorisation for availing the treatment on a cashless basis as per procedures laid down and in the prescribed form. Please read the policy document as soon as you receive it to familiarise yourself with the process rather than wait for a claim to arise.

Claims on reimbursement basis

Read the clause relating to claims in your policy document as soon as you receive it to ensure that you understand the procedure and the documents required for making a claim on reimbursement basis. When a claim arises you should inform the insurance company as per procedures required. After hospitalisation, you have to ensure that you obtain and keep ready documents such as claim form, discharge summary, prescriptions and bills that you should submit for a claim.

KNOWLEDGE BYTE-4

RIGHTS AND RESPONSIBILITIES OF PATIENTS

Patients' rights in India Highlights

1. Right to information
2. Right to records and reports
3. Right to Emergency Medical Care
4. Right to informed consent
5. Right to confidentiality, human dignity and privacy
6. Right to second opinion
7. Right to transparency in rates, and care according to prescribed rates wherever relevant
8. Right to nondiscrimination
9. Right to safety and quality care according to standards
10. Right to choose alternative treatment options if available

11. Right to choose source for obtaining medicines or tests
12. Right to proper referral and transfer, which is free from perverse commercial influences
13. Right to protection for patients involved in clinical trials
14. Right to protection of participants involved in biomedical and health research
15. Right to take discharge of patient, or receive body of deceased from hospital
16. Right to Patient Education
17. Right to be heard and seek redressal

Responsibilities of patients and caretakers

Along with promoting their rights, patients and caretakers should follow their responsibilities so that hospitals and doctors can perform their work satisfactorily:

1. Patients should provide all required health related information to their doctor, in response to the doctor's queries without concealing any relevant information, so that diagnosis and treatment can be facilitated.
2. Patients should cooperate with the doctor during examination, diagnostic tests and treatment, and should follow doctor's advice, while keeping in view their right to participate in decision making related to treatment.
3. Patients should follow all instructions regarding appointment time, cooperate with hospital staff and fellow patients, avoid creating disturbance to other patients, and maintain cleanliness in the hospital.

4. Patients should respect the dignity of the doctor and other hospital staff as human beings and as professionals. Whatever the grievance may be, patients/caregivers should not resort to violence in any form and damage or destroy any property of the hospital or the service provider.
5. The Patients should take responsibility for their actions based on choices made regarding treatment options, and in case they refuse treatment.

(Source: http://clinicalestablishments.gov.in/

CONCLUSION

After reading this book, you might have started thinking about "how to make you and your family live more happy, meaningful and fulfilling life." I will provide you the way out as it is my responsibility to make you secure from the onslaught of diseases, and not to end the book on information count only. You can get information from anywhere. I am sure, you have not picked my book only for information.

I want to make this book a launching pad for your complete health and wellness. Rest assure, this book will open a floodgate of health-related opportunities for you and your loved ones and empower you to throw all the health-related woes to the wind.

ANNEXURE

Now registered free* for Electronic Health Records service by visiting – MDHL – My Digital Health Locker (https://app.mdhl.in/)

Or

Download the MDHL – My Digital Health Locker mobile application from play store or app store.

How does it work?

Step 1: Register and Login with https://app.mdhl.in/get your unique MDHL I'd

Step 2: Print own Health Card [which will have your Name, Address, Age, emergency contact details, blood group, Mini Health History (allergies, blood pressure, diabetes...), Health

Insurance policy name and number, etc.], to carry your complete health records in your pocket/mobile.

Step 3: Upload all the records onto the secured digital Health Locker. In order to scan the documents, simply take a picture of them.

Or

Request your healthcare providers (or yourself) to Email all the health records to your unique MDHL I'd.

Step 4: Approve the Health records (to avoid spams).

Step 5: Whenever you need to access your medical records online, sign in or just enter your details to access them. You can view your personal health records online on the https://app.mdhl.in/

In case of emergency your healthcare providers can access the same if you allow (through OTP).

Road to Buy Best Health Insurance:

1. Determine your current needs
2. Understand expenses you can afford can't afford
3. Decide the members to be covered
4. Fill detailed information to view comparison and quotes
5. Research insurer and verify network hospitals and benefits
6. Buy the selected policy
7. Renew the policy on-time to avail benefits.

Making a Health Insurance Claim

Steps	Planned	Emergency	Reimbursement Policy
1	Go to the hospital and present your insurance card	Get admitted to hospital. Present insurance card.	Get admitted to hospital. Present insurance card.
2	Hospital coordinates with insurers	Hospital treats you.	Hospital treats you.
3	Insurers ask documents from Hospital		You pay the hospital bills.
4	Insurer authorize the procedure in line with your policy		Insurer ask for complete treatment records
5	You get treatment		Insurer ask for all invoices and receipt of the payment made
6	Insurers settle claim and bills		Insurers settle claim and reimburse according to Health policy

Prescriptions Abbreviations: https://hemangpajwani.com/

List of Insurance Company in India: https://www.irdai.gov.in/

Blood bank list of India: https://cdsco.gov.in/

Links to download forms for Organ Donation: https://www.notto.gov.in/

SOURCES

https://fit.thequint.com/
https://friends2support.org/
https://www.kokilabenhospital.com/
https://www.stmaryskc.com/
http://clinicalestablishments.gov.in/
https://www.thebetterindia.com/
https://www.indiatoday.in/
https://www.notto.gov.in/
https://en.wikipedia.org/
https://blogs.medibuddy.in/
https://www.quora.com/
https://www.cdc.gov/
https://blogs.webmd.com/
https://medlineplus.gov/
https://www.apollopharmacy.in/
https://www.pittsburghhealthcarereport.com/
https://www.drugs.com/
https://healthengine.com.au/
https://www.verywellhealth.com/
https://www.quora.com/
https://www.surgeryencyclopedia.com/
https://www.gethealthystayhealthy.com/
https://www.truenorthitg.com/
https://www.healthit.gov/
https://www.mayoclinic.org/
https://www.webmd.com/
https://capo.wildapricot.org/
http://www.bccancer.bc.ca/
https://www.moneycontrol.com/
https://mdhl/in

www.ingramcontent.com/pod-product-compliance
Ingram Content Group UK Ltd.
Pitfield, Milton Keynes, MK11 3LW, UK
UKHW021654190726
13853UKWH00001B/260